Easy Does It

First published April 1990.

ISBN: 0-89486-673-7

Printed in the United States of America.

ABOUT P. K. HALLINAN

Patrick Hallinan began writing children's books at the request of his wife, who asked him to create an original Christmas gift for their two young sons. Today, nearly twenty years later, P. K. Hallinan is one of America's foremost authors of children's books that teach personal values and self-esteem to young readers. His sensitive text and heartwarming illustrations offer a celebration of life to all who visit his very special world.

Although Mr. Hallinan writes primarily for children, his books manage to touch the child in all of us. It's this ability that enables Hallinan's books to be enjoyed by all children, young and old, who see the world through the eyes of innocence.

Mr. Hallinan lives with his wife, Jeanne, and their three dogs in Ashland, Oregon. *Easy Does It* is his twenty-sixth children's book, including *One Day at a Time*, published by Hazelden Educational Materials.

Easy Does It

P.K. Hallinan

HAZELDEN®

Easy Does It

For Sid

Just go nice and easy,
it's all you need do
to handle the story
that life writes for you.

You can sing a nice song
when things go all wrong...

or laugh till you cry
when things go awry.

You can even go fishing
and let yourself dream
as life's little worries
go floating downstream.

Just go nice and easy,
it's the very best way
to capture the rapture
of each passing day.

There's time to pick flowers
and time to chase clouds.

There's time, too, for wandering
and pondering aloud.

When you go nice and easy,
it's simple to see
that life's biggest lesson
is just learning to BE.

You don't have to win
at each game you try.

And you don't have to soar
when you can't even fly.

Winning and losing
are all in your mind;
if you go nice and easy,
you'll win every time.

You can take a long walk
if you feel less than par...

or have a long talk
with the moon and the stars.

Your troubles will fade
like late April snow
if you give each one up
when it's time to let go.

Yes, time is a present
that rolls on forever.
It leads us through sunshine
and, sometimes, bad weather.

But everything happens
the way that it should—
and everything's guided
by Infinite Good.

You don't have to worry
when things don't go right.
There's always a morning
to follow the night.

And try to remember
that this too shall pass...

and we all take turns
being first and last.

So take your own time,
and set your own pace.

You're bound to succeed
if you run your own race.

Yes, life will be brighter
from beginning to end—
Just go nice and easy, and...

Easy does it, my friend!